Dec. 2005   Whitechapel

For   Bernadette
   Good luck & everything
      David Church

      020 7790 0269

O the Windows of the Bookshop Must Be Broken

David Kessel

Collected Poems 1970 – 2006

Survivors' Press

First published in 2006
by Survivors' Press
Studio 11
Bickerton House
25 – 27 Bickerton Road
London N19 5JT
www.survivorspoetry.com

Copyright David Kessel © 2006

This book is published with the financial assistance of the Esmée Fairbairn Foundation

Designed and typeset in Minion Pro by Survivors' Press
Printed and bound in England by Onedigital, Brighton

Edited by Alan Morrison © 2006
Cover design, layout, typesetting: Alan Morrison © 2006
Proofing: Roy Holland

ISBN 1-874595-06-2
ISBN 978-1-874595-06-9

A catalogue record for this book is available from the British Library

David Kessel is hereby identified as author
of this work in accordance with the Section 77 of the Copyright,
Designs and Patents Act 1988

This book is sold subject to the condition that it shall not, by way of trade or otherwise, be lent, resold, hired out or otherwise circulated without the author's prior consent in any form of binding or cover other than that in which it is published and without a similar condition including this condition being imposed on the subsequent purchaser.

All rights reserved

A CIP record for this book is available
from the British Library

Acknowledgements

David Kessel has been published in *City Limits*, Hackney Writers Workshop anthologies (1980s), *Phoenix Co-Operative* and *Poetry Express*, in which he regularly appears (featured poet in Issue 20).

Five of his poems were read by actor Joe Powell in the EMFEB Symphony Orchestra's performance of composer Owen Bourne's 25-minute score *Hackney Chambers* at the Salisbury Hotel, London on 5 November 2005.

Anthology credits:

Bricklight: Poems from the Labour Movement in East London	Pluto Press, 1980, Ed. Chris Searle
Under The Asylum Tree	Survivors' Press, 1995
Outsider Poems	David Amery 1999
Orphans of Albion	Survivors'/Sixties Press, 2006

Previous publications:

The Ivy	Aldgate Press, 1989
The Ivy, Collected Poems 1970-1994	Aldgate Press, 2nd edition, 1994

Survivors' Poetry would also like to thank Hilary Hodgson and the Esmée Fairbairn Foundation for providing the funds to produce this volume through the Survivors' Poetry National Mentoring Scheme 2005-06.

Contents

Preface: 'Storming Heaven in a Book': A Poet of Compassion	7
Emily Brontë	19
Glass Is Dynamite	20
Songs of Soho	22
To the International Brigade	25
For Desmond Trotter	26
The Ivy	27
Across the City Grey Clouds Heavy with Rain	28
Simple Poem	30
Broadstairs Beach on Jubilee Day	31
From Hell to Hackney	32
Fragment	33
Hungering	34
Beautiful Ireland	36
Search For A Mate	39
Intimacy	41
In Memory of Jude	42
In A Southern English Seaside Town	43
The River	44
Willesden High St	45
On Broadstairs Beach	46
New Cross	47
The Tree	48
Woman Stone	49
Desire	50
In Finsbury Circus	51
One Body, One Soul	52
Extension to Sidney Keyes	54
Disintegration	55
England, O England	56
Elegy For Lost Innocence	58
Possessed	59
In North London	60
How To Dance	61
Desperate Sex	62
For Emma, Aged 10	63

Bus No 253	64
The Barren Age	65
Autumn-by-Sea	67
For Drummond Allison	68
A Mug of Black Coffee	69
For Zoe	70
Commonground	71
The Weald	72
The Hungry Heart	73
The Songthrush	74
Paranoia or Stupidity	75
Ireland	76
The Park	77
Arnhem	78
Disgusting Times	79
Mike Mosley	80
Schizoid	81
Limehouse	82
Man Stone	83
To Bleed With Her	84
The Fisherman	85
Inheritance	86
Over the Top	87
Life Poem	88
The Vixen	89
London	90
Poetry and Poverty	91
The Stillness	92
Life Against Death	93
Summer Rain	94
Human Hope and Hackney	95
Tough One	96
Hillside, Llangattock	97
Notes on Schizophrenia – *The Utopianism of the Schizophrenic*	98

A Fragment

A poem by Peggy Kessel

'Storming Heaven in a Book':
A Poet of Compassion

To say it is as much a privilege to know Kessel the man as it is to know Kessel the poet is to deviate from the true task of a literary preface, but bearing in mind the essential humanity of Kessel's work, I think it is germane to express this. Kessel's personal qualities of humility and sincerity are all the more striking in light of the chronic paranoid schizophrenia from which he has suffered since his first breakdown at 17. He is now 57.

On first meeting Kessel in 2004, I sensed palpable inner struggles when greeted by a shy, vulnerable man with large pained eyes, *Jude the Obscure*'s 'Little Time' grown up – gaze on the photo of Kessel as a boy on this cover and you will see depicted a harrowed-eyed version of Jude Fawley's troubled son; a precocious sense of moral responsibility burdening his brow like that fictional twisted innocent. And responsibility is one thing Kessel the poet never shirks: he writes with naked honesty of the brutal truths on the psychological front line. There is a genuine analogue here: the trauma of schizophrenic breakdown expressed as a metaphorical shell shock, its symptoms the shrapnel from breakdown's abstract battlefield.

Indeed, in his spiderishly scribbled letters to me over the last year, Kessel has often quoted Wilfred Owen: 'Poetry is a savage war' – as well as Joseph Conrad, from *Lord Jim*: 'In the destructive element immerse'. This too Kessel does, fearlessly. He takes much inspiration and spiritual strength from the sentiments of the soldier poets of both world wars: Charles Sorley, Drummond Allison, Sidney Keyes, and his personal favourite, the inimitably barbed Keith Douglas. On one of my visits to Kessel's flat in Whitechapel, he showed me his treasured spine-cracked edition of Keith Douglas's Complete Works (replete with brittle brown dust-jacket), intricately inscribed with cramped notes framing each poem; and as you will see, some of Kessel's poems begin with Douglas quotes. Stylistically and expressively however, Kessel's poetry has more in common with that of Ivor Gurney and, in particular, Isaac Rosenberg. Interestingly Kessel's cultural background shares similarities with the latter: while Rosenberg was the son of a Russian-Jewish immigrant who settled in London's East End, Kessel is the grandson of a Jewish tailor of German-Jewish ancestry ('kessel' is German for 'kettle') who emigrated from South Africa to North London. Kessel has also lived in the East End since he was 24.

Kessel's familial background is, in his own mind, indelibly etched in his psychological make-up: with a Jewish tailor grandfather on his father's side and a Blackshirt poet grandfather on his mother's, Kessel himself thinks it a truism that he has been more susceptible to schizophrenic symptoms than most. This poses an intriguing genetic theory on the illness, and Kessel is ever the self-analyst (see *The Utopianism of the Schizophrenic* on page 98). His parents too play crucial roles in both his psychology and his poetry. His father is the field-surgeon Lippy in 'Arnhem' (page 78), whose experiences of war obviously heightened Kessel's idiomatic identification with war and its poetics; and his mother, who converted from Catholicism to Communism during World War II, presumably had some influence on Kessel's own politics (discussed later) and indeed his poetics – gifts she inherited from her oppositely political father – as evident in a piece of her verse printed on her son's request at the back of this book. It is arguable that the fusing of a Blackshirt's poetic impulses with the polarised social awareness of a Jewish immigrant has resulted in the leftwing polemical outpouring of the poet grandson.

I first came across Kessel's work when thumbing through the poetry collections for review when I started at Survivors' Poetry: his hefty chapbook, *The Ivy – Collected Poems 1970-1994*, with its inside quotes from Edith Södergran and Christopher Caudwell and absent contents page instantly intrigued me, as did the heartfelt Preface by the author himself; and the empathic introduction by the late Arthur Clegg (reproduced on the back of this book) with its emphasis on David as a 'poet of compassion'. After reading this generous selection of consistently powerful and emotionally challenging poems (which I reviewed in *Poetry Express* Issue 20), several words competed in trying to sum up his intensely expressive style: 'raw', 'ragged', 'visceral', 'spiritual', 'polemical', 'bitter', 'contused', 'bruising', 'inspiring', 'lyrical', 'imagistic', 'onanistic', 'political', and so on. But perhaps the word which best summed up Kessel's work was that chosen by Clegg: 'compassionate'. Whatever one thinks of this poetry, few can deny the almost tangible spirit of compassion – a disappointed and enraged one perhaps – seething through practically every poem. This is demonstrably a poet who cares deeply for people and for the 'Broken city' macrocosm in which he observes his fellow beings (or Londoners), as if peering into a bustling rock-pool from which he himself is, for a multitude of reasons, separate yet attached; an anomic anemone. And a Cockney cockle: throughout his poems he alludes to an almost semi-mystical motif of the 'Cockney', apparently embodying his aspiration for a true 20th/21st century, self-possessing working-class identity – a macro-Cockney. Consciously or unconsciously he perhaps also alludes to the label which fictionally broke the will of John Keats (who was more thick-skinned than posterity gives him credit for): a poet of the 'Cockney School' – the snobbish drubbing by John Wilson Croker in *Blackwood's* magazine, April 1818.

On first reading Kessel I was struck by the frequent ideological references littering his work. In the very first poem in *The Ivy's* sequence, 'Arnhem' – a war-inspired piece strongly reminiscent of Siegfried Sassoon and Keith Douglas* – erupts the line 'Down to fifty and like Lilburne won't be beaten', signifying a political significance in the choice of this 17th century Leveller* as a symbol of defiance. Clearly this was a poet whose sympathies lay on the Left. A few pages on, 'To The International Brigade' further cemented a – noticeably historic – leftist erudition. 'Beautiful Ireland' proffered the equally telling reference to Robert 'Tressel' ((sic): the single 'l' misspelling, an unconscious mirroring of 'Kessel'?), author of the British Left's favourite work of fiction, *The Ragged Trousered Philanthropists*, as a figure of 'passionate commitment'. In 'Songs of Soho' Kessel openly expresses his ideological aspirations, albeit slightly obliquely: 'Will I and my world-joining hope of Socialism be drowned in this lusting ocean?' And the almost incantatory 'For Zoe' is littered with other telling tributes as Kessel – almost reminiscent of the late Ian Dury and his nostalgia-loaded pop lyrics (i.e. 'Reasons to be Cheerful Part 3') – lists the 'things' (human and inanimate) that inspire him: 'Keir Hardie's eyes', 'Robert Tressel's (sic) passion'. There is also, at the front of this collection, the beautiful quote from the granite-willed Nye Bevan along with one from British Marxist Christopher Caudwell and a reference to the Burford Levellers; into the collection, two poem-accompanying quotes from Edgell Rickword, veteran of the World War I Artists Rifles and Socialist poet, including his striking "That forward blasting vision love"; and a dedication to the late Michael Robinson, 'London teacher, anti-racist and Communist'.

A poet of the underdog, the outsider, the societally-labelled failure, under-achiever, or purely fate-thwarted, Kessel carries a torch for those unhappy numbers among whom he no doubt – and unfairly – counts himself; a willing martyrdom on behalf of the disenfranchised side of the Us and Them equation. He writes of the posthumous known, both real

---

* It was Keith Douglas's generation whom – exactly 300 years to the month after Lilburne was impeached by the Committee of Examinations for arguing for religious tolerance on 17th May 1645 – voted in the leftwing members of the Commonwealth Party (led by demob-bed wing commanders), which in their four bi-election wins in May 1945 forced the resultant Attlee Labour Government into a far more radical leftwing programme of reform than it had previously contemplated under the likes of its manifesto drafter Herbert Morrison.

and fictional: Robert Tressell (unjustly unpublished in his lifetime because the publishers refused to read his manuscript in long hand); Thomas Hardy's Jude (*the Obscure*) Fawley ('In Memory of Jude'), rejected by Christminster University on account of his lowly social status; and lesser known 'obscuritans' (this writer's term for individuals unrecognised in their lifetimes) such as Mike Mosley, 'Grey, calloused, forgotten at fifty', and Kessel's late friend Harold Mingham to whom he dedicated *The Ivy*, lauding him as 'a great working-class poet'. Might we then say that Kessel's poetry is Socialist: that of today's true, forgotten working-classes scribbling fugitive lyrics in East End tenements? Well, we might. There's certainly a strong sense of solidarity, artistic and social, surging through his poems. He quite clearly lays out his poetic manifesto in the polemic 'Poetry and Poverty' (originally published in *Outsider Poems*, 1999):

> The poetry of the common people has been driven underground since 1660.
> Poetry and otherness; the otherness of the common people.
> When we cease to share, our language becomes a cipher, the language of the
> despatch box and the popular press.
> Towards a new lyricism we need to rediscover a deciduous language, that of
> Winstanley and Emily Brontë.
> There can be no cockney power without cockney poetry.

This Leveller-style manifesto – far more than mere agitprop – focuses typically on Kessel's 'Cockney' motif, marrying historical and contemporary working-class political culture by implying the natural inheritors of working-class lyrical polemic were the pop songwriters of the punk era:

> Cockney poetry is underground poetry expressed in Rock music; downbeat, dissonant, demotic; e.g. The Clash, The Jam, The Free.

Certainly there's some truth in this: how many poets – or even songwriters for that matter – of the last twenty years have written about urban hardship or social alienation? Well Kessel is one, but he's certainly in a minority (bar Tony Harrison and Pete Morgan, I struggle to think of many others). Occasionally one might be reminded of, say, The Jam's Paul Weller-penned lyrics such as 'Down in the Tube Station at Midnight', 'That's Entertainment' and 'Town Called Malice' (1977-82)** when traversing Kessel's urban

---

** Weller's late poet friend Dave Waller inspired many of his early lyrics, essentially pop poems, in particular the fictional future civil war concept for The Jam's 1979 LP *Setting Sons*; Weller also included a stanza from Shelley's 'The Mask of Anarchy' on the rear sleeve of 1980's *Sound Affects* album.

inventories (both writers echoing Blake's London-centricity), indicative of a definite punk flavour to his poetry; that bittersweet blend of social nihilism in the face of unaccountable consumer culture, mingled with a surprising leftwing optimism; Modism rather than Modernism. And like the punk-Mod ideologists of the late Seventies, Kessel thinks there is another way for us to live, and certainly not 'the third way'. He still clings to the second: Socialism.

It's also in this polemical piece that inevitably emerges that other great 17th century proto-Socialist, Gerrard Winstanley, leader of the Diggers. There is indeed something of the social pamphleteer in Kessel, which is one way of summing him up: a militant poet polemicist. And in a similar spirit to the inimitable, mainstream-bashing tirades of Sixties Press poet and polemical pamphleteer Barry Tebb, the uncrowned laureate of Leeds (also at heart an urban-Romantic), Kessel (the pearly-crowned Cockney laureate) makes no bones about his contempt for the contemporary poetry 'establishment':

> Established poets are idiots and liars,
> also by definition great poets sleep in gutters
> love is pure contingency
> the eyes are everything.
> ('Schizoid')

The more fractured and oblique 'Glass Is Dynamite' however is the true polemical *tour de force* of Kessel's poems. It is dedicated to Virginia Woolf, Joseph Conrad and, most fittingly, T.S. Eliot: the piece certainly echoes aspects of the latter's apocalyptic masterwork, *The Wasteland*. The poem seethes with frustrated yet efficacious creative force and offers the strikingly anarchic Rimbaudian rallying cry: 'O the windows of the bookshop must be broken' (the inevitable title for an inevitable collection). On one of my visits to Kessel's Whitechapel digs I asked him what he meant by this extraordinary line, and he replied: "The only things that were alive in Hampstead were the books in a shop I went into. I thought, the windows of the bookshop must be broken, so the books can spill into the streets".

Poverty is an integral theme throughout Kessel's poetry, nowadays perceived as 'the poet in the garret cliché' by a largely suburban mainstream. Yet we all know only too well how un-lucrative poetry is, especially today, so why the surprise that some poets, especially un-established ones, live in similar material hardships to the Chattertons and Davidsons (cue his anthemic 'Thirty Bob a Week') of yesteryear? And that given, why not write about it? Anyone who has experienced poverty will strongly empathise with such themes, and anyone who has not might well learn much from attempting to; and what better means than through the naked self-expression of poetry? Perhaps in Blair's 'progressive society' we like to pretend poverty doesn't really exist, or just happens to other people, certainly not to reasonably well-educated verse-scribblers. But let's not forget that not all 'poets' living today hail from Oxbridge or the conveyor-belts of the UEA: there are also the state-educated 'naifs' (to use one of Simon Jenner's idioms), the Redbricks, blue-overalls and pinstripe poets (those who hold down ordinary jobs and write in their spare time) and occasional isolated autodidacts who slip through the net into some measure of public consciousness. You could do a lot worse than Kessel for swatting up on the material hardships some inspired minds scrimp in:

> A deadly man with loveless breath.
> Time eating the stomach. Can't afford fags.
>   ('Disintegration')

> We live with uncertainty,
> our giros and our dreams.
>   ('New Cross')

Kessel has often related to me his own take on Keats's Negative Capability ("...when a man is capable of being in uncertainties ... without any irritable reaching after fact and reason" – Keats, 1817): he describes his poetic ethos essentially as 'anti-intellect'. I have taken this to mean Kessel believes in putting the heart, soul and guts back into poetry, and steering it away from the cerebral extremities of some Modernists; those Don Paterson for one has referred to as 'obscurantists'. But perhaps Kessel's true target should be the 'populists' – as Paterson terms the mainstream poets –, many of whom arguably indulge too much in the plain and mundane, the apolitical 'just-so-ness' of society, the preoccupation with 'things' and 'tangibles' to the neglect of 'ideas', 'abstracts', 'phantasms' (i.e. the imagination); whose conscious attitudinal postures, or Poetical Correctness, might take heed – along with their polar opposite 'obscurantists' – of Keith Douglas's humanistic dictum cited by Kessel as the source of his own poetic ethic: "'Bullshit' – it is an army word, and signifies humbug and unnecessary detail. It symbolises what I think must be got rid of – the mass of irrelevancies, of 'attitudes', 'approaches', propaganda, ivory towers etc., that stands between us and our problems and what we have to do about them" (from a letter to JC Hall, August 1943)***. This viewpoint is echoed in Kessel's 'Beautiful Ireland': 'If I could cut out my bullshit intellectualism/ as easily as I crap in heather/ there would be no more wars or leaders'. Kessel also says of his Douglas-inspired humanist emotionalism: "The invaluable purpose of poetry is to create hope in difficult circumstances****, which manifests in the significance of the British war poets. Standing where people, creatures, things hunger. Being essential, how few are the things that are really essential".

Modernists (and even 'populists') might scoff at Kessel's somewhat 'naïf', cathartic style, spitting out the term 'confessional', apparently a contemporary insult. But surely the urge to express oneself is in some sense synonymous with the urge to confess? Or is it just the Catholic poets among us – practising or lapsed – who feel this urge to purge themselves through poetry? And do we take it that they are currently doing so in a climate of Protestant Poetics? A personal communion with the Muse not to be communicated publicly until transubstantiated into a palatable and rational draft; a trend for individualistic as opposed to socialistic subject; a preoccupation with private perceptions and issues as opposed to public and political ones? In that case, rage on the Recusant School.

No poets would espouse wilful 'obscurantism' – a conscious closing-up to the general readership through a semantic esotericism that only the most erudite of eyes can decode – yet certain types of Modernist poetry can be (mis-)interpreted this way. Equally it is difficult to believe that any adherents to the more pellucid mainstream would champion dull diction and flat prosiness of form, yet many are undeniably guilty of this. Striking the right balance between metaphoric colour and emotional directness is the steepest hill for any poet to climb, but I think Kessel has come close to reaching this elusive summit, in spite of his work's somewhat ragged, imperfectionist qualities. Kessel expresses his emotions nakedly and uncompromisingly in combination with metaphor and evocation, the nerve and fibre of poetry. He combines the visceral with the spiritual instinctively, producing work which is both innocent and experienced at the same time:

*** It's interesting to contrast this with Keats's comments on Haydon and Horace Smith in the same letter of 1817 which proffered his theory of Negative Capability: "These men say things which make one start, without making one feel; they are all alike; their manners are alike; they all know fashionables".

**** similar to the definition of Modism: 'striving to be respectable in difficult circumstances'; in the Mods' case this manifests sartorially, in Kessel's case, poetically

> The church is harder than my desire
> though much less real,
> as hard as my patronising lust,
> and so I masturbate in the wet grass.
>
> ('Beautiful Ireland')

Kessel's 'anti-intellect' stance might be doing his work a disservice in that such a self-label detracts from the demonstrative intellect pulsing through it. One is led to conclude this is a deliberately contentious claim on his part, a necessary exaggeration or over-emphasis to get an essential, humanistic point across to those who might brush off less absolute phraseology. Kessel's intellectual gifts are as evident as his expressive ones, his poems littered with tantalising aphorisms and metaphors:

> The rain is falling
> on chipshop and battlefield.
>
> ('For Drummond Allison')

> A rasping melody of charlady morning challenges conscience.
>
> ('Songs of Soho')

> Eyes melting like song in the evening street.
>
> ('In North London')

> Listening to the soft rain on the leaves
> I hear the decency and realism of friends' humour...

> I who am as dangerous as these cliffs
> strive to be as kind as the meadow...

> I fear this mountain I must climb more
> than I fear fascism in a loved-one's eyes.
>
> ('Beautiful Ireland')

> Today a sweetheart's sigh is more dangerous
> than massed armies.
>
> ('Desperate Sex')

> A bored mouse storming heaven in a book,
> the look took all my caring.
>
> ('The Ivy')

Combined with this accomplished imagism is a gritty Romanticism, a sometimes breathtaking Shelleyan lyricism – often punctuated with the Kesselite sing-song, exclamatory O – all the more striking for its post-industrial backdrops:

> O to share a fag on wintry evenings
> in a lonely street – all iron and sleet.
>> ('To Bleed With Her')

> The piano scatters wide her mournful seed.
>> ('In a Southern English Seaside Town')

> And I'll follow the night-train to distant starved cities
> to bleed and pain and sing
>> ('Bus No 253')

> Hancock and Lennon have passed through here without being heard
> to find peace in the burning innermost slums.
>> ('The Barren Age,
>> For the Londoners of my Generation')

> Despair in a girl's heart, where wild
> chrysanthemums should be.
>> ('Disintegration')

Kessel's striking descriptiveness is painterly, his poems often resembling figurative word-pictures, with an expressionistic quality echoing Lowry's moth-toned cityscapes of industrial drudgery and Van Gogh's tangible vividness:

> Anger at love that disturbs the malicious street
> leaping in the gutter with petrol and stubbed fags.
> the rusty smell of the sea and misogynists' guilt…
>> ('A Mug of Black Coffee')

> A Cockney cleaner moves home eastwards
> into the bright slums of humanity
>> ('In Finsbury Circus');

> A rasping melody of char-lady morning challenges the conscience.
> …a drunk's daydreams break across unfamiliar streets.
>> ('Songs of Soho')

> These silent clouds between silent rows of Brockley terraces.
> … To meet this earth in full flight
> between its suicide and the market-place café.
>> ('The Park')

There's an unfashionably visionary element to Kessel's poetry, harking back to Blake's schizophrenic epiphanies (for example *Songs of Innocence*'s 'The Ecchoing Green'; 'Holy Thursday' and *Experience*'s 'The Chimney Sweeper'; 'London' – see Kessel's 'Elegy For Lost Innocence', page 58) in its to-ing and fro-ing between polarities of social realism (charladies, bus workers, cockneys and so on) and bucolic utopianism; and William Morris's aphorisms of romantic utilitarianism and the intrinsic beauty in the useful:

> For there is within the soul of labour the tenderness
> of the violet beneath the shaking lonely chestnut.
> ('For Emma, Aged 10')

> Tender words and arms by a spitting gas-fire.
> Before the triumph of tyranny on the television
> dreaming of news from nowhere
> ('England, O England')

> ...the summer smell of lilac from a scrapyard.
> ('Willesden High Street')

Whatever one's critical judgement of Kessel's poetry, one can't deny that it reeks of truth. In other words, Kessel is a sincere poet, he 'feels what he feels' as Arthur Clegg said, and not 'because it might suit an audience'. Anyone who has had the privilege of listening to Kessel reading his work will have been struck by the impassioned, almost prophet-like manner in which he loudly howls out his poems, as if each word robs him of strength from the weight of its significance to him. The truth, as it is to him, is in his words. And like all truth, it is both painful and empowering. Despite the palpable sense of struggle and conflict in Kessel's poetry, one does ultimately salvage from it a sense of optimism and empowerment, for this poet is still here, still writing, still battling the same lifetime's demons, but those demons have failed to beat him into mute submission. Contrarily, they have driven him out into the world of others along the same steep-verged path trampled by the likes of Clare, Smart, Crane, Mew and Lafitte before him, through the liberating power of self-expression. His poetry climbs from its circumstances and pillages them for inspiration, producing something far more lasting and permanent, and beautiful.

Alan Morrison, March 2006

This book is dedicated to my late friends Pat Ellis, who saved my life, and Harold Mingham, a great working-class poet, and to my son, Tom

'Pain gives us all we need,
Love, Solitude and the face of death'
Edith Södergran

'Freedom is the possiblities of becoming'
Christopher Caudwell

'When I am surrounded by enemies,
I close my eyes and think of the poor'
Nye Bevan

'Thompson, Perkins, Church'
The Burford Martyrs

Emily Brontë

Stone-head straight up
in the flower-bed
quarry-man to the
adoration
of purple and yellow
too long turned in
under the rocky-hearted soil

Orange
weeps into flowers
that she only
between lonely sky and cold earth
stands with it
within the grey quarry-stone
burning

Stone-age dreading stone
cries out for colour,
come wind and thunder
one by one
tear petals asunder.
seeds of raped flowers
down through soil of centuries
plundering

Pity the grey-axed wind
for the yellow-brained sun's sake.
Pity the grey stone
for the purple-hearted violet's sake.

For the sake of the seeding of orange
in the grey soil suffering
the stony poetess grows,
in a tomb
within a people
whose violets
flourish
only in its graveyard

1970

Glass Is Dynamite

Dedicated to T.S. Eliot, Virginia Woolf and Joseph Conrad
– wide windows of the old world

'The new world shines through all the windows of the old one'
Lenin

Glass is dynamite
in Hampstead on the hill even the bricks are made of glass
and the books are prisms, primed with
His Wasteland
Her Lighthouse
His Sailors
but the mirrored eyes that pass see themselves only.

Glass is dynamite beyond the heath where only his solitary
nightingale hears the cries from the fearful deep,
across the ponds where the fisherboy alone may enter
the all-breaking sea,
down, down into the grey ocean pitching with drowned young sailors.

In Hampstead on the hill only the bricks know the terror of their
drowning
and only the books are dreaming of the drowned ocean,
and the mirrored eyes that pass are waiting
to see themselves
only

O the windows of the bookshop must be broken.

Now staring eyes
His Wasteland
Her Lighthouse
His Sailors
escaping down beyond the heath and ponds into the ocean.

Can it be true,
this learned demolition-man
mortaring bricks
in the callous ocean?

Can it be,
her fragile beam that's breaking
into the fathomless worlds that lie between
the chanting waves of drowned young sailors?

Can it be true,
this reflection through the long mist
of the wrecked imagination
a figure rigged with ropes and sails that his mates have cleated
standing out of the pitch-black sea?

The fisherboy stands as the voyage begins
and the nightingale stops to hear the song
of the new Magellan.

An adumbration
of versing young sailors,
kindling
out of the stony rubbish
bright lilacs.

Back on the hill they're growing vines
to hide the bricks of Keats's cottage,
but the windows are exploding.

1971

Songs of Soho

'Adam in me, in you Eve fears to tread
a world not moulded in the heart's desire'
                Edgell Rickword, 'Poet to Punk'

Do the Songs of Soho sell good food and sex,
the easy things men like when they race into chaos?
Is this the Playland where we touch but can't trust magic thrills?
Is this the sound made when an emptied head bangs on a hollow world?
Can the good wine of the city be the wide-ringing voice of the apple seller?
And is it also the sparrow, whose song may be sung within?

The photo doesn't show what tarts up the shy Sicilian girl.
Green as young oranges when she came awkwardly to these streets
strange as her customs are narrow to us.
Something devious about the roses here makes an earthquake
in the childhood garden where she'd heard spring birds
and when alone she sings her sad, fragmented songs
we throw her stares like harsh flashing pennies.
Our suggestions like neon scar the meaning of her tears.
Then she learns the hopelessness in our easy laughter; fancy
flower that's forgotten home's provincial evergreen.
O what makes it seem that she is not assaulted?
She's singing now in empty shaded groves, her mind
out of the terrible sun of her solicitous night.

Step inside gentlemen, leave your guilty minds;
sit in the warm and worldly lap of your genesis.
The hounded brain obeys, kills the rhythm in the blood.

What makes George believe he can only sing in her secret holy passage
when his song is for us all in a frank, generous sky?
After the hurried act, leaving the pain of the world unmoved.
He lingers in bright alleys with the well-respected fuck.
Does he mistake its vigour for his freedom – is he too unsure
to chance it behind her eyes? Unsung, ordinary
love – the steel of freedom – jeered at
by the winking eye of a cynical world.
The dirty old man murdered by sterile lust in these streets.

Step inside gentlemen, dull your guilty minds;
sit in the warm and worldly lap of your genesis.
The hounded brain obeys, kills the rhythm in the blood.

Along exotic pavements a youth tramples his confused soul.
Can the music he finds be welcoming the chaos of change
to move but not to change, to sing but not to alter.
The image of himself is his cool and desperate hope.
When he finds himself different, in a new light,
he gives this stranger a ticket to an anonymous side-show,
so no-one will see him with a strange love, forgets
where he has come from. Fearfully pockets his soul.
By the slot machines of the Crystal Room his leaping notes ring bells
and impressively turn lights on within reflecting walls.
Kept inside glass his songs are surrounded by night;
his sun shut-in burns a hole in his heart.

Step inside gentlemen, forget your guilty minds;
sit in the warm and worldly lap of your genesis.
The hounded brain obeys, kills the rhythm in the blood.

Now he never stops trying to bed his genesis, being so holy, with his
                                                                                                                           dreams
desperately he fucks the world-green sweetness out of himself,
O but he was born also from the midst of growing, ravaged forests,
the cold winds, rains, stones of rough-diamond Nature.
Will I and my world-joining hope of Socialism be drowned in this lusting
                                                                                                                           ocean?
Never more the pained soul's angry leap to the loving edge
of an inchoate, curiously open world?
Between the difficult need and easy solace there can be no communion;
I must fight my lust yielding a song of sweet struggle;
in the arms of the universe find the liberty of my becoming.

Fierce-loving bells of St. Martin's are tolling
against the difficult cause of Man-bound history.
Perhaps if we could ring out from within the frail
unspoken substance of that to-be-died-for meaning
in our hearts, our songs would carry us to Heaven?
I dearly hope when dead to spend eternity in Hell,

for when with comrades in these streets we do not sing the Internationale
our painful thoughts disturb the arguments of brotherhood therein.

Out of weeping shadows the persistent drumming
of bitter strangers from the downtrodden Orient mock us.
Through bloodless streets we hurry home, to bury our heads
before the rosy raucous dawn of neglected brothers.

A rasping melody of charlady morning challenges conscience.
One day her acid rain will scour Soho
and men see themselves cut-up in its razor light.

Now the hellish throbbing's stopped.
A drunk's daydreams break across unfamiliar streets,
and a songthrush wakes his mournful love for Ireland.

Why can't he take his daily threnody with milk?
He observing the gentile flowers of Soho Square through a haze of insult
fallen with conforming hours, would find them stunning funny,
but their blooms aren't worth bleeding for by their thorns.
This evil animated by his grin simplifies the stubborn world.
O once when the city's smirking stars are out he'll dig up his garden
and plant the soft wild Irish flowers that bloom on tears.

Now Candy she's waking choked with our consuming narrow passion,
and he must numb the throbbing void with whiskey.
Here we all become outcast; English with Chinese and Italian.
If we could form a choir, our one and many voices
would pluck the heartstrings of London.
The suffering Cockney must make, with tunes and whistles,
tough worldly songs of anger, irony and hope.

1972

To the International Brigade

What was this rabble doing here?
Miners, poets,
poet-miners.
They leave their stars and bones
with ungentled plains
and in the blood of the Asturias.

1972

For Desmond Trotter

Will the Queen be hanging Desmond Trotter,
knight the freedom fighter?
We English it is well known are very fair,
even on holiday we'll see justice done,
horizon-drunk, ocean sat-upon, native girl plucked:
tyranny ripening in our minds like fruit.

Strung between the royal past and the plebeian future, a youth,
all black between the sea and the sun.

Back home bitter we contemplate our rotting state;
then to dreams silent as snow, sick with sweetness.
The moaning world outside like a great flowing tide
staked-round with guns and secrecy, briars and blindness.
Death leaps from Dominica to Hackney keen as daylight;

I stumble out into my back-garden, where snowdrops swing
black as the earth-trapped spring.

1974

Desmond Trotter was leader of the Unemployed Young Workers' Movement in Dominica, which then in 1974 was a British protectorate. He was framed on a murder charge and sentenced to death. The Movement for Colonial Freedom, in which I was involved as meeting organiser, eventually had him acquitted, although he was finally given a life sentence.

The Ivy

For Wendy

'The unmoved poet walking the crazed moon'
                                 Sidney Keyes

That house holds all my care.
A woman nursed my confidence there and I found through her flesh
the surviving spirit in my mess.
This is the way I was.
A bored mouse storming heaven in a book,
the look took all my caring.
This lunacy I bespoke upon a wan and desperate hope.
The view from a window
upon a playful ground was mine in lieu of wanting,
and in the eyes of working men I met a worthier ken.
Violence in the soul
was change and ghoul,
and my heart was stolen
by her hair, auburn and oceanic.
The men, their arms and hearts, were all I knew
and if I slew it was for them,
their knowledge and their giving.
Now I am this blood without a body,
mysterious sight and seedless;
sexual in the night, fleshless.
With this light I'll turn my back
and a rendering I'll make of heaven
and hell, and bleeding.

1975

Across the City Grey Clouds Heavy With Rain

Greater by far than the glass cathedrals of Capital,
beyond the horizon of our most firm investment,
a foreign seaman stands in lowest Stepney.
Wearily he plumbs his good friend the river
to work out his heavy life in its dumb depths.
His bitterness says more than all sophistication.
Rather the raging sea than our smart society!
O to celebrate his hopes beneath an estuary sky.

I'd give half my life to have you in my arms.
What I must do is more difficult than this.
Besides circumstances, must overcome such deadly
diffidence, work through such moral complexity.
Inward workings stubborner than tenements.

Each of us is Dante, our Hell is here.
Our love leads us through a burnt village
and the city's wasted minds.
When in each other's arms we lose ourselves
a hungry tide will gain from our charged souls
and in the hating eye of a man starved of vision
we can make our children.

O I need your love to rivet me to this world.
Roots to feel, air to sing,
joy to struggle.

Spring in the neglected graveyard.
Such resurgence from so much lingering death!
I lie a while between broken stones and bindweed,
watch a thrush nest-make, think how sweet flowers
love most to twine around rustiest barbs.
A simple kindness greater than all gods.
Here with untamed dogs and weeds I dream
of making a child with the woman I love.
O to sing out as clearly as the blackbird does
above the din of Mile End. But human love is a quiet

constant labour of consideration and hope.
A passing train tells me that this can be
a beginning, I rise vigorously.

The rain unites us. Through the city pooling
light, behind a million eyes in empty streets.
In bar and teashop sombre minds turn
to curious humour daring day's tight nerves.
Diffidence drained by the giving sky.
Corner of mouth and eye speak of that other sun,
so homewards swirling with everything.

1977

Simple Poem

Our land made by us
through strangest history.

Seaward hoping.

After work find ourselves
in joining streets.

Hungry for freedom!

We need horizons
beyond trying days.

Many things make us
skilled and social;
kind mates, open skies,
the passages of love.

White-boned, black-blooded
and green as spring allotments.

Dawn across the city;
our longing to reach to the world.

1977

Broadstairs Beach on Jubilee Day

Let the anthem slip quietly into the sea.
The gull cries more about our birthright.
By the wind we know this passing flag,
celebrate the wind, unfailing with rain and
seaward liberty that never bled an empire.
The beach is marked by the history of everything.
Kids sense this – digging, building, sifting, destroying;
on a Bank Holiday we can even find ourselves.
By our modest love we may know the swell and dangers of our tide,
our curious scope beneath vast changing skies.

The outward keening eye will not always be pawned
to the past and stupid obsequy, it shall break free.
Unfathomed inner seas shall stir
with worthier beckoning worlds.
Child, turn to face another and the ocean
grey, gold and leveller green.
New horizons shall choir in you
as ages old and to come meet where your foot treads in the sand.

1977

From Hell to Hackney

Hold ground
carry cruelty's curse quietly inside
in all back streets and neglected
space of our cities
constantly rebel like spring.

Surrender's sweet murder
for daylight in the soul
like it or not
hold the universe within
to kill is to kill all

deader than desert dust
rather than let our blood trickle
into a wooden heart
it can sweeten fucking hell
if we stand straight
here where we should.

Keith learnt to drink terror
in the morning, with a sigh
swallowing the tight system
in his dry throat,
a most serious young explorer
of our golden oasis

War's lusting.
Bled into mature sands
he calmed deadly authority
inside; as strange flowers do
in callow heat. Attacking
like lead into the back

I will never mention the terror
I prospect, considering our
future. But seek to determine
all living in itself
what I do now well and simply
is my religion.

1978

Fragment

I am part of all this: I will drive
me through my paranoia till I bleed.
My gashed love is one with the scarred hills
a changing sky and the broken city.
I am as dangerous as these cliffs
and I strive to be as kind as the valley.
Your fear binds me with your dense wonder,
you the swirling water in which
I seek to drown myself.

1979

Hungering

While I awkwardly roll a fag
a robin sings from a holly tree.

It is we who fence ourselves in.
Like foxes we hunger underground.

The rowan thrives in fierce winds.
The wind brings it rain, bears its leaves and fruit.

I pick a blackberry and find a worm.
I leave it to eat the flesh
so the pips may lie naked on the ground.

I turn my female god naturally
into this beetle on my hand.
Then with love I can watch it.
I'll go on making such magic till I die.

On harsh and bitter ground
nettles grow abundantly tall.
Cows make sweet milk from them.

In a sacred wood
I dream of life's conception.

This hawk in a tree hungers for life.
This jet-fighter for death.

If we were really like sheep
we would not kill one another
nor slaughter other animals.

I listen to an owl's ironic hooting.
It knows well its strength
but kills only what it needs.
Thus I will survive life's harshest winter.

To be a sea-trout seeking a mate
at the stream's head.
I would live with her as wagtails do
independently by the stream.

The rain is falling into our valley of life and death,
falling on mankind's disintegration of cruelty.

The path becomes a muddy stream.
This is the way I see a woman I love
moving in her freedom with the dark purity of earth.

Sometimes I feel like the bare sky
longing for the earth.

I have climbed this hill to learn to care.

1979/80

Beautiful Ireland

'I am possessed
The house whose wall contains the dark strife
The arguments of hell with heaven –'
                  Keith Douglas, 'Landscape with Figures'

Growing to hate my self-absorbed, diffident past;
a hate born of simple kindness and deeper understanding,
all really good things take time to emerge.
Such is it with my gentle passion, which
as I come to believe in it I'll use
to go like Gorky into this world,
openly, anonymously with the people.
With the passionate commitment of Emily Brontë
or Robert Tressel*, I could enter
the terrible marrow of my age,
seeking peace, unity, simplicity. And I
such an intense, complex, divided person.

Tramping an Irish road I think of the woman
I love, and of her lover, and by my boots beating
the tarmac of their intimacy. With my longing
I conceive the men who laboured to make this road
and the women who made that possible,
their union and children.
The rain is falling, the kind rain,
and I, alone, sit beneath a tree,
the magnificence of which I cannot describe.

Closing my eyes I dream of making love
to a girl from the last village, standing-up
against the altar of her church and facing
the Virgin Mary. The church is harder
than my desire, though much less real,
as hard as my patronising lust,
and so I masturbate in the wet grass.
By doing this I feel myself ordinary, mortal,
fertile; my inner natural holiness.

Listening to the soft rain on the leaves
I hear the decency and realism of friends' humour
and looking up into a grey sky
watch a heron slowly fly across the field;
such a purposeful, self-possessed creature.
How could a man-like God create this magnificent life?

On the road I pass a pair of ducks,
perfect in themselves and with each other.
I who become a callous god by eating their flesh,
their united carnality and spirituality,
try to hold my hunger gently in my eyes.
O for simple intimate mutuality with a woman;
to unfold with ruthless equality ourselves within each other
and in everything we do and say; and by
our children, who must be themselves, learn to help others.
Become as helpful and selfless as the rain.

O Ireland, whose kind people and soft hills
survive bigoted churches and bloody landlordism,
butchered pigs are still the backbone of your nation.
In a pub I make an advance to a girl.
Running away across a field I am confused;
too long I've been running from my sexual passion
from fear of violating my parents' sacred love.
I turn back, resolving to possess it
within my seriousness and reserve.

I fear this mountain I must climb
more than I fear fascism in a loved-one's eyes.
Through intimacy with its bold, durable nakedness
I come to know my own disintegrity
and my terror of becoming mad.
Worse than the fear of death, torture, rejection.
O mountain, climbing you by a difficult route
and slowly is a study in becoming kind.
Up into the peat-bog and the wind.
If I could cut out my bullshit intellectualism
as easily as I crap in the heather
there would be no more wars or leaders.

Beneath a rowan I feel the usurped earth;
this is why man has abused his mother
and his sisters. The clouds stir my limbs.
What in the heart of this rock-sky unites
my tired will with my weak aching body?

Hope is like this falcon hunting over the valley;
keen as the eye which hungers for life.
When common folk have grip on this world
we shall be this bee in the heather.
This suffering stone longs for the wind, rain and stars;
my burning blood for love and justice.
A view of the valley, distant hills and sea
is where the stone's hope joins a people's thought.

To become pure we must rebel,
hate murderous duty and blinding pride.
Never on our knees except before
the hopeless, the suffering and the sky.
O to bridge the terrible seas of bigotry,
raped Ireland and the self-obsessed English.
I who am dangerous as these cliffs
strive to be kind as the meadow.
By the scarred rock-face of my thought
I shall remain true to my love,
though without you I cannot be faithful.
You in whose swirling waters I would drown
so becoming free to walk naked in my cruel city.
Love that makes impotent men sing in streets with joy
and long-suffering women bleed with kindness.

August 1980

[Note: *[sic] – see preface]

Search For A Mate

The eyes of a woman I love
are a living hell.
As deadly to an earnest explorer
as they can be fruitful.

If kindness is worshipping
love-making is pure expiation.

The gulf between longing and uniting
is as difficult as any sea.
Enter in it with expectation
and I'll surely drown.

I do not lightly hold the gun between my thighs.
I am a callow thing, can kill with ease
the keen feeling brain that communicates.
Her 'Yes' as desperate as my will
in her vagina incinerates all hopes.

Eros crushed by dad's bullshitting,
for fifteen years I sought to free myself
with shy prurience in streets and parks
boldly aching in my single bed:
insane ways
to enter her complete, to be strong
within her, to find myself.

Now I'm learning frankness simply: fucking
the bourgeois and sexist religion of fucking,
fucking the system everywhere I can.
I find my potency in fallen leaves
and make love smoking with a tramp.
With planetary determination I
carry my seed in my eyes.

And of her, heavenly stranger,
I long to know each hellish detail

of the possibilities of her own becoming.

To struggle with all my strength in Hell.

Tomorrow I'll meet her eyes with the terror
and hope of an insurgent in Auschwitz.

July 1980

Intimacy

It seems we've come this far quite alone
and our suffering has burnt our insides out.

I'm handed a joint in a square next to a fountain
where youths wash their feet and throw rubbish.

I prefer to suffer than to dream,
to burn within indelibly as spring.

The youths chat to each other painlessly,
smoking and dreaming without pity.

The moon's no need of us. We live
by our strange inner electricity.

My need to be with a kind woman breathes
on the good stone beneath calm, noble trees.

Thin rock music from the café. A dog
with desperate eyes searches for food.

Facing despair within would make the square
aflame with suppressed tendencies and truth.

A drunk kicks a bottle, talks to everyone.
A girl laughs. A quiet man stares at the stone.

We may help the dog and the drunk.
If we care, their naked hunger can

flower in us, deep and disturbing.
Though, with longing, we may never touch.

Love can break us open into untold spaces
between the trash and the trees, knowing

the oneness of ourselves, and with the stone,
the simple dead and the passionate unborn.

1982

In Memory of Jude

You could still marvel at the blackbird singing
above the dusk college square with sombre bells
ringing beneath May sycamores.
At bookshops bleeding with mankind and the firmament.
Fancy youths with death in their hearts
pass up and down the seductive streets
and behind thick walls make words deadly
with expectation and fear, drunk with themselves.
Only in the cold churches they struggle
to win some divine life.
The desperate vagrant is more solid:
he remembers, as yourself, the rich flinty earth,
cuckoo calling, smell of wheat in rain on a down.
Your death's carved in stone in library windows.
Your tears angry, soulful music in a pub
by the bus-station. Beneath a bus
your sweetheart wrestles with uncertainty,
spanner in hand, her poems in her pocket.
You are the busman, bright-eyed, eager to know
your mother's dark land. Your children's children
may enter this city with nothing but strong
boots, good bread and hope to destroy
and create a strange people's history.

Oxford, 1982

In A Southern English Seaside Town

For My Grandmother Emmie

I

The waves are breaking.
Black and white water collide
in a man, steeled to the making
of an English rose garden.

The sky is breaking.
Grey and gold armies hurled
into a soul, fearful for the turning
of his own nurtured soil.

A mind is breaking.
O what briary headland may
enter his heart, with the ebb and flow
of a new becoming?

II

An old woman is searching
for the redolence of her summer garden.
Beneath the circling gulls she grieves
a lost rhapsody, the men who are at sea.

Rachmaninov, a yearning song,
summer friends who are lost and gone.
In a guest-house a grandchild dabbles and smokes
knowing inalienable wrong.

The horizon holds her unutterable need,
listless terraces her loneliness,
inward sailing to fearless continents.
The piano scatters wide her mournful seed.

1984

The River

For Andrew Gleadall

Freedom from self is the greatest freedom
across the arguing river.
Your golden web must sing in the tributary of despair
with broken spirit and holy rock.
This is the way it was before man first raped his sister
out of anger with his poverty,
and will be after the last lust's spent.
Love is human responsibility
and the raging of the moon over Brixton Streets.
You in a backstreet pub where Blacks play pool and dominoes
and sing lowly of labour and lost earth;
with your girl drinking rough red wine,
learning Jamaican brogue with an old chippie
bleeding into your souls;
the bitter dark bleeding and the aching inner light.
Bidding goodnight in tipsy Cockney
your room dimly lit and spare with Dylan music
a dog barking in a hungry street
the terrible bond of cunt-love whereby
a man learns to walk the grey giving savage waters.
And I am waiting for a Cockney Turner
to paint the London streets with nobility and guts.

1984

Willesden High Street

For Ted Young

I don't know whether I found first
red roses at dusk
or a blackbird at daybreak.
Dirty walls like broken grieving.
The hunger of heaven in this laboured street.
Aching love for mum, thirsty beneath a black sky.
Youth's desperate meaning, the asylum of childhood.
From the sorcery of a pub, a Gaelic lament,
sex given for blood in damp rooms,
a sacrament holier than sacred broken bread.
How can we live without our memories where
the bestridden gutter meets tired workers and a savage sky?
The possessed cries of lovers behind the graveyard
and the summer smell of lilac from a scrapyard.

1984

On Broadstairs Beach

The smell of common stock with wild iris on the headland.
In the terraces, slow cancerous Edwardian deaths.
Heedless kids fathom the breezy surf,
whilst the aged wise sift eternity within the all-membering sea.
The gull speaks of ocean-tide love-grief;
a curious child longs to know the salt in her depths.
At the parade's end genteel folk sit sipping champagne;
what blindness is it that they cannot tell
how like the brine it is?
The salt wind and the sun over Africa bring life
to this land of dense beauty and blind subtle bigotry.
What Salvationists with what melodies can bring liberty
and loving sight to our bitter blinded land?
Winter is coming to these northern climes:
a long, hard, bitter terrible bloody winter.

A quizzical Cockney searches the uncertain horizon
for hope. Tide ebbing over wondrous deathly terrain.

July 1984

New Cross

For John Van

We build our own slums. The wind
through the slums blows on the highest
hills. We are all slowly dying
of cold and loneliness, no fags,
no fruit juice, and neighbours with veg stew
and cups of tea. We live with uncertainty,
our giros and our dreams. Yet our aggression
is our frustrated love. In a billion painful
ways we make the little things of love;
a dustman's sweat, a cleaner's arthritis,
a streetlight's mined electricity,
a carpet-layer's emphysema,
a desperate clerk's angina,
a mate's slow moaned caresses.

1984

The Tree

For those suffering from schizophrenia

Steady flesh rooted in misery.
Against the purpose of the city.
Sap shattering mirrors in men's eyes,
into the still source of tears.
Crusted, robbed and knotted into
a broken-wide sky.
Tormented nobility, with
budding as serious as grief.
Leafy galaxies
out of divided, unlevelled earth.
Naked resurrection
between terror, hatred and despair.

1985

Women Stone

Worked in wonderment, out of nebulae.
On three sides laid-open by ice;

perpetually awaiting the rain's love.
Miracled below where a rough-hewn
edge meets her naked giving quick.
She gives her hope, womb-dark and
crystalline to the terrified leveret
through a half-moon sensual eye.

Wounded by the stars, bleeding
milk. Deep in bracken, nurturing
animal sleep and the dawn light.
Pained and selfless in a fen
and within the splintered streets of cities,
the illumined core of the cosmos.

1985

Desire

In gratitude of London bus workers

What makes fear into trust in the beginning?
Hunger is half of life, and death in the afternoon only
another beginning: "Love is a wilderness" on bleak
November Sundays, emerging from terrace
and tenement to walk with fearful dreamy kids,
pints of bitter and crying gulls.

People are curious sexual things.
We free one another in queues and beds;
never turning from suffering, heartache in our eyes,
beyond the fence to the westerly hills.

A black couple climbing, blood and death
in their clasped hands, children in moist eyes,
to the high hill's windy brow. A calm view
of honeyed meadows echoing in the blood.
The dying sun miracled in each other's tired limbs.
The long stint homeward with cider in our veins.

When desire turns to deadly expectation
in dowdy avenues, in small back rooms,
take the stuttering heart and the trembling hand,
and pace the horizon with aching shoulders,
dead golden leaves and fantastic moons
in the gutters. Rather an unremembered ant
than a fulsome pimp, a dispassionate heart
in a cold terrible sea; to die for her
without rooting her. To face death we have
to face bloody Arnhem, the high desperate,
demanding, diabolical mind with the withering smile;
gutting numbness in brothel, paper and betting shop;
a baby's shrieking, embodied cosmic terror;
the terribility of love on wet and windy mornings.

October 1985

In Finsbury Circus

This tree can teach me a lot if I let it
but am I ripe for it?
I am callow, cold-hearted and confused
but ripe for a gentle awakening
there is death all around – walking,
discordant, fearful death.
The tree has bargained its frail, beautiful leaves
with our death-dealing;
the friendly sparrow, its song with our hard hearts;
a drunk, his wise, telling talk with shilling and pence.
What they teach me I burn against this human winter.
The deadly demanding director has rendered his blood
for a strange imperial glory.
The tree and the drunk are breathing deeply.
What do we need besides murder and victory!
A Cockney cleaner moves homes eastwards
into the bright slums of humanity.

1985

One Body, One Soul

*In memory of Michael Robinson –
London teacher, anti-racist and Communist*

Black, grey and white, O pigeon you are
the true citizen of this city, with that passionate sheen
that Cockney youth have in Brixton and Bethnal Green –
ours is a city of psychopaths and punks,
layabouts and night-cleaners, pathetic bankers,
lovely busmen. I in my summer guilt prefer
quiet anonymity. Yet there are few who are
innocents here, a few poor and black kids
roaming the streets without racial lusting
and sexual envy. Still with black and brown
worlds under us: feeding us, nurturing us,
sustaining us body and soul in the parks
of Kensington, and tenements of Bermondsey.

Bitterness of fag-smoke at the back of the throat
incites us to vital knowledge of violence, despair:
bursting flower-bed and teeming supermarket tended
by a burnt African village and craving Irish stomach;
shrivelled eyes of Indian children speak
of cuppa' after cuppa' in the local café;
a Jamaican labours for the stone in our fireplace;
Chinese sacrifice for our holiday binges.
Angrily, I stub my fag out with my foot.

There's a bench on Hackney Downs where one
can watch half the world: a woman drudging
heavy bags from the market, an old man
with pockets full of confused memories,
a Cockney lad – angry, brave and silent;
green English common between sombre estates.
At night, lovers beneath a wild indifferent moon.

O, one day our stubbornness must break away,
for it cannot endure the changing needs
of our indestructibility

And the pigeons join us as we step along and down
the streets together, singing, piping, dancing,
beneath spreading plane-trees.

1985

Extension to Sidney Keyes

Blessed amongst the angels of the gutter.
As the water in the fountain seeks aid from the dark
overwhelming sky. Only the cripple knows the bleakness
of the statue, the barrenness of the square without nature,
without naivety for the despairing girl, her magnificence
looming from the temple tower, to die for her child's sake.
Madness through the evening air. How to suffer workscorned day
without Irish soul? Eyes creeping to loins with
hope of our future, scratching the genitals of marble.
The beaten road and the high, desperate State.
Derelict on the grass, the determination of worms turns
southwards to the sun. Songs are as hopeful
as the giving heart, milk in the hand. Peace,
like the peace of three a.m. dreams in deafening night.

September 1985

Disintegration

Vagrant
'Which of us will catch tears in the simple hand"

Ten minutes in a littered street. Lead
in the mind; police-sirens gutting the blood.
Smart people fumbling, ordered by inane voice.
Perversity in the heart, the redolence of a magnificent
September turned to prurience in the dust.
"Living in an ice-cage". Sexual
frustration like fag-smoke in the aorta.
Despair in a girl's heart, where wild
chrysanthemums should be. Desire in the heart,
gutting anger. Telling vision against people.
A deadly man with loveless breath.
Time eating the stomach. Can't afford fags.
A derelict person lies stretched to the leaves.
To pick up a mate beneath a star-filled sky.

September 1985

England, O England

For Hilda and Ray Sims

Corruption of the majesty of a spring morning
in wild, lowly meadows. Helvellyn is God,
and the smell of hay in distant lanes.
Within unyielding cities, lost broken people seek
Daisy and Tom in dirty corners.
Expropriation of the heart of an English girl
in the pitiless bed, desire levelled to
the beaten pavement. "Love is wilderness", and truth
grows with the flowering willowherb on wasteground.
A youth done down with insurance against life
in concrete glass above the innocent slums and river.
Electricity through noon air, breathing blood.
Indolence in backyards, unused spades, untethered
chrysanthemums burning the stars in dowdy avenues,
a sky where hope lingers, grips the burdened heart,
the dusty blood dreaming in the gutter with the warmth
of mum and dad at conceptual work.
Apple pie and custard, bitter tea and aching love
in the grey clouds beyond the window. A friendly
café in Ladbroke Grove, chatting, listening
for the lilt in a mate's breath. Eating good chips
with an old man on wintry afternoons, dusk in his mind.
Earning rent on cold corrupted sites, willing fingers
bent to bitter graft with brick and cold earth.
Grey geese winging a darkening sky over
the railway. Meditation at maniac crossroads,
rolling fag-smoke. O God that you made
such beautiful women; tough, worldly and gentle
in the face of violent filth. Slowly wandering lonely
streets on the homeward stint, fearful of poverty
and war, dishonesty and lies, to the windswept
door of birth, fellowship and luck.
Purity without innocence in a mate's kitchen,
cauliflower and stew, smells of washing, lending
two hands. The beckoning and bewilderment of children.

Tender words and arms by a spitting gas-fire.
Before the triumph of tyranny on the television
dreaming of news from nowhere.
Drudgery of a Welsh girl in a cold fetid cottage,
hopeless dark in her belly, desire wrenched
in her slow blood, raking the sky with her tears.
Exploitation of the heart of a Norman boy
in savage wily villages; Hell in the afternoon
on a cold hillside, iron in his hand,
terror in his belly, a dying fire in his heart.
Children playing with pebbles and moonlight on wild beaches.
Porpoises swimming westward beneath December stars.

November 1985

Elegy For Lost Innocence

For Celia and John Lee

Take the burdened eye and bitter
heart, and pace the withered ground
with desperate step. The hand is sound
and aching guts are commoner.

Our nation lives on stolen time
and virgins see the masks of hate,
yet hunger lingers at the gate.
We prepare for a world of mime.

Lost is the blessedness of the street.
Come back to where the grass grows wild
and rooting men are sweet and mild.
Ours is the terrible love we'll meet.

This our broken perjured land
made fulsome by a terrible sea,
earth rendered for a twisted fee
before a bent and working hand.

December 1985

Possessed

'She could be a bird, a dead man, a photograph'

Leaves die golden on the burdened earth.
Understand the jewel on the bitter ground.
Trees are shitless and the giving wind knows
great despair. There is great hunger in the fallen
leaved vein, and purity in the savaged frond.
This flesh delivers the gravel to fragments
of dreams. The sparrows feed on these, to sing
on beaten pavements through the vicious winter.
The moon knows the vicarious sexuality
of the frost-bound stone, watering February spring.
The crocus bleeds with all this furious marrowed sorrow.

December 1985

In North London

The drunk's spat stuttered Celtic song on
the North London line, though Hell has a savage
beauty more rending than the sea glens of Argyle.
For God's invincible peace he is afraid.
Beyond the train a wild sky and a hard, broken city.
How to communicate our dire, tender sexual
curiosity in this great and bloody city?
A young sycamore growing out of a Cola tin;
two girls talking by fags and moonlight;
two men drinking bitter with dark fear;
a woman searching rubbish for an evening meal;
a couple with bitter truth in their eyes.
Eyes melting like a song in the evening street
reach pitiful corners of labour and silence.
In the highroads, traffic terrorises searching hearts.

1986

How to Dance

An elegy for Keith Douglas

'To do this is drilling the mind'

Our terrible sex hungers for deliverance.
A laugh of Londoners lingers on
our bitter hearts, yearning for
the stars in the street, beckoning or
tearful for cows and pigs within.
These are the pavements of our inheritance.

Snapping our fingers in pubs and backrooms
the dense blood explores our deepest
texture. Our voices sing in the wild
cosmos plenty with bitter and mild
creatures, and we yearn to quest
the pity of the deadly in our moons.

Time hangs heavy in our working limbs.
We lose our hearts in each other's
moistening eyes, and wander
savages infinite eternity in fear
and music to the limitless sisters
of birth and death and sadness.

1986

Desperate Sex
A Fragment

Have you ever seen the naked beach tree
on open downland in December?

The manliest man I know is impotent.

Today a sweetheart's sigh is more dangerous
than massed armies.

I wish I was a Cockney lad
with a sweetheart on my arm
my aching heart's last leap from
the gutter to your moist eyes.

1986

For Emma, Aged 10

'That forward blasting vision love'
     Edgell Rickword

With the wind over June corn
the railwayman's hunger knows the loneliness
of the chestnut in the corner of the field.

Men can and will destroy the flowers of spring,
taking their tenderness for time,
their petals for forbidden hunger.

Go swimming in high June rivers;
climb northern hills in August;
tramp the streets of your great broken city;
sit in cafes with old folk and tough hearty youths;
talk gently in the evening with a young sweetheart

till you find that land which Edward Thomas knew
between the bloody trenches and the marble mansions.
O the glory of that kneaded, furrowed, tortured land.

And what is greater than a stone
but the linnet in a peasant woman's heart.

Learn the railwayman's great hunger
that knows no self,
only the wind and stone and fellowship.
Scorn the vanity of useless men.
For there is within the soul of labour the tenderness
of the violet beneath the shaking lonely chestnut.

June 1986

Bus No 253

O woman on the top of the bus
you've stolen my heart.
A nurse, careworn and upright, knitting
between Whitechapel and Hackney.
I've a dream tonight of a child
playful and serious,
learning through us the bittersweet world
with a frown and a chuckle.
I know now something of a love beyond words
which the blackbird learnt at dawn aeons since
and which I can bear with pain till the light
falls silently from my wrecked body.
You have made beechwood of my heart
and magic of my blood
and I'll follow the night-train to distant starved cities
to bleed and pain and sing.

June 1986

The Barren Age

For the Londoners of my generation

'If you could love me, love me bravely'
                      Miklos Radnoti

Spiritual hunger rules our land
till the crofted north breaks wide the sky.
The cowed dog hounds sheep on southern down
and callow youth lust for comfort and blood.
I in my dividedness long for a Negro blues
to bring tears of regeneration to our savage city.
The stinted heart plies for its love alone
shuffling streets with abuse and dead hands.
Hancock and Lennon have passed through here
without being heard, to find peace in
burning innermost slums. I in my June
guilt know some of the sources of this sorrow
and crave for Hancock and Lennon to break
wide the desperate streets with laughter and weeping.
Dying November sunlight across the river,
O God did you intend this city to make us mad
before our own destruction? Sadness driven
underground. Destroying the sexual pity
of true men and women. O for a fierce
loving fuck inhabiting the night.

Between terror and love lie our sweethearts
gun-running for the Blacks on a rainy night,
in an ambush with our forefather's flintlock
on Islington Green. Due north north-west
our hope lies with wild hills and magnificent women.
John MacLean's children born of genocide,
in cold slums, without work, learn alike
respect for women, men, children and the crippled.
And across the sea, John Mitchel's children,
the passionate people of Dublin.

I who have seen Richard II, Uncle Vanya and O'Casey
know something of this sorrow, its burden and its joy.

Ray Sims and Rugiero Grieco came out of the earth
like apple blossom to lay their eyes
on the poor, the indolent, and the hated bosom.
Evening sunlight over the distant Hebrides
and a dunlin crying on a savage shore.

August 1986

Ray Sims and Rugiero Grieco were proletarian Communists who organised the disorganised workers and peasants of West London and the south of Italy in the 1940s and 1950s.

Autumn-by-Sea

In memory of my mother Peggy

Breaking waves teach us
the torture of dark distant lands
and our own blind needs.

All war and peace in headland gale caught
in the face, the rapture and villainy
of a cross-grained land.

A pebble turns in the surf dense as a star,
bright as Armageddon, cold as cod, turns to the sun
to fathom its hapless unspeakable wrath.

A searching threnody of gulls across a blinded town.

A blackbird in a headland laburnum sings of honour
yielding the depth and infinitude of our stolen world.

On the beach youths surge and cry
plying their futures with darkening horizons.

In November twilight an old man spades
roses against fierce winds, humming
a tune his father learnt on the Somme.
His pity rakes the terrible sky with June.

November 1986

For Drummond Allison

The rain is falling within, bitter rain.
Bitterness is our food, rusted iron,
and the savage cries of geese over a grey river.
The bullet that stopped you turned your rusted words
into crying songs for these icy dissonant years;
heathland across our corrupt splintered cities.
The corruption of the flesh and the purity of a race
long-since guilty of rape and double-dealing
in desperate high-streets and iron fields,
lives of crass expectation and bloody illusions
in emblemed homes fenced against the planetary wind
and the sighing earth. The rain is falling
on chipshop and battlefield, and the estuary
of your pain flows worldly into the gulled ocean.

1987

A Mug of Black Coffee

A listless fury in my right foot.
A greasy bacon butty in June hail
and the fervour of dogs fornicating in the park.
Anger at love that disturbs the malicious street
leaping in the gutter with petrol and stubbed fags.
The rusty smell of the sea and misogynists' guilt
in a laden heart, where the split ego flows over curious shingles.
A dying carnation in a tea-shop. Grief for a lost
darling and a smile for the wide-eyed courageous waitress.
Pizza pie and sad rock across the zany
divided town, and a savage lamenting westerly.

May 1987

For Zoe

I would give you
Keir Hardie's eyes
the woods of Raasay
Charlotte Bronte's care
the smell of stock in Haworth churchyard
Fred my brickie friend's hands
the song of a blackbird over Clerkenwell
Robert Tressel's* passion
rough Somerset cider and cheddar
Bengali children playing in Spitalfields
summer rain over Stepney
the tenor sax of Lester Young
sparrows nesting in a Hackney tenement
the Bothy band
the revolutionaries of Ireland
a Yiddish love song
herons flying across a Norfolk fen.

July 1987

[Note: [sic] * see preface]

Commonground

For Liz Wright, Irish peasant woman

Sleet on the skin beneath a grey arched sky.
Salt on the tongue and painful hobbed feet.
A thin sun beyond a fallowed field.
Hands on cold iron for bloody beet.
A hungry mare licks her foal.
Crying children share a crust.
A thrush sings in the dusk from a sycamore.
Women hoe turnips for a night stew.
A vixen barking from a hawthorn copse.
An old man rolls harsh-cut tobacco.
A waning moon over lopped poplars.
A stick fire under a briar hedge.
Rabbits staring into the twilight.
A lonely song from a hunched body.
The silence of crows making homeward.
A tired youth climbing a rusty bike.
The chatter of hedge-sparrows in a bramble bush.
The smell of ash-smoke from a greasy hearth.
Dirty children playing with tea.
Sad women mashing swedes.
A gust of wind through a cracked window.
A man handling lumps of coal.
A bare bulb from a blackened ceiling.
A thin cat nursing kittens.
A white wall with Millet's 'Gleaners'.
A rotten bench with a stitched cushion.
A boy strumming a broken guitar.
A mouse terrified for bread.
A girl noble as Della Francesca's Madonna.
The foraging of a badger in a potato mound.

1987

The Weald

Lines in memory of Keith Douglas

Sink yourself in the earth, its rough
grit, its bitterness, its worm-milked leaf.
Feel the clod between bent fingers
and the harrowed clay within old shoes.
The line of the earth against the evening sky.
Breaking bread beneath a pollard willow
a hedger dreams a hard broken land;
in his face a March wind and the cry of the lapwing
over the marsh. Before he was born he lived
with a crow. In this bare field, sleet
in his eyes and stones in his gizzard.
The crow's halting low, warning flight his midwife.
as a kid he fished in the ditch with stern mind;
now grimly he plods the dark rainy field
listening to rabbit, owl, vixen.
In rough hands he grips a barren time
and a gutting winter, and lays bare
a field of rape and his grey, bare home.
O the hate and the love for his chill, grafted home.

1988

The Hungry Heart

For the people of Poplar

The rowan flowers in lowest Poplar
for the gaunt hacking northern sailor.

Travellers cry like Pavarotti
across the streets where they are feared and wondered.

Old men stumble into noon light rubbing
their eyes with aching stomachs and dreams.

Women chatter to church bells where
the heart's dark water swells.

Children play with seaward wind and bread
and toss each other strange wild words.

A man grasps tough hands of
suffering and trust and six a.m. graft.

Resting his load on a woman's eyes
who could change his life in a night.

Plain Michael Faraday brought down the sun
to clean the house and have some fun.

In the 'Hope & Anchor' darts and words come
alive to turn heads and break wide the sky.

Tired at night strange limbs entwine
in the rhythm of the river and the stars.

1988

The Songthrush

From a dead tree a song stark and steadfast as solitude.
I have known some friendship but none like this aching
dark terrible singing across a small plot at dusk
betraying our humanity with its pitiful desire where
meeting the night beckons desperate cottages surrender
to the roving wind and hawthorn copses' nurture.

July 1988

Paranoia or Stupidity
(Being the conjunction of my oddness with the oddness of the universe)

'mixed with good signs, and all received with levity,
or indifference, by the amazed mind'
                      Keith Douglas, 'Negative Information'

Being alone and inaccessible is a difficult thing
more so in these trying days of Gestapo lingo
and pubs full of concentration camp guards.
I'm not scared of being hurt or killed
but deeply distrust the closing time and space,
the rush to comment, the gush to relate.
I fear direct identification, the winning smile.
Symbolism rules this nation: a whisper heard
on a street, a caricature of my sexuality;
another abusive look at a workman in the road;
a glance of death into sad eyes
where the living struggle for tears;
a dissonant nudge on the bus
when one dreams of making love;
sworn at when I talk to a vagrant;
the conjunction of a car revving up
with belly sigh of longing;
sirens and moonlight.

A land of murderers and gardeners
made unholy by dereliction
I prefer to find life in the warmth of a few words shared,
chance acquaintance of bindweed with a rusted railing.
I will face the future with the blankness of the unknown
and the full vivid protean present.

February 1989

Ireland

In a Kerry bus station jackdaws eat rubbish;
an old Republican carries plastic bags
weighted with friendship and old ham.
The hills bequeath the memories of the Troubles
and a longing for young blooded boots. Great
age has made this land schizophrenic
with Deirdre's love and Kilkenny races; suffering
suffering in old faithful faces, and affluent contempt.

The cars run on slaughtered pigs. A man
who carried a gun now has a hacking cough.
On bended knees this land lives, hard
slog and the crack at street corners.
A whistled song and the jackdaw soaring
over misogyny and open serious faces.

July 1990

The Park

'Blind, hungry, unwept, insensate,
To our unutterable faith we wait'
                        Charles Sorley

It's my manhood I'm scared of: will they destroy
this Black man with the beautiful eyes walking his dog
on a calm spring afternoon in Brockley Park?
My father stole my balls for the tears of battle!
This is the London I'll remember in my dreams,
this little park between sturdy ageing Victorian terraces.
Why do I feel guilty of my sex
in this wooded valley overlooking our grasping city?
A calm red-haired woman reading intently on the grass.
I guess it's my fury with my brother!
I meet the future in that Black man's eyes.
I go in search of a raging hunger to meet
these silent clouds between silent rows of Brockley terraces.
This is the way it was before I was corrupted
by cant, double-dealing and leadenness
to meet this earth in full flight between
its suicide and the market-place café,
and the Black man's eyes and the woman's nobility
in an alleyway on the sweet walk home.

April 1990

Arnhem
In memory of my father, Lippy, a battlefront surgeon at Arnhem

Tommy dropped and copped the lot; Hitler, Churchill, Stalin.
'No use' he thought, his inalienable Anglian guts lying across his sten;
uncanny how he felt no pain in his dying guts, only
an unbearable pain in his heart for his Suffolk Daisy.
'No use Tommy' the Dutch nurse said calmly, passionately
caressing his fingers.
'Uncanny' the crow thought, as it watched the fourth battalion
being mown down north of the railway line,
'How the best of humanity are murdered for nothing'.
At the fatal bridge a dying corporal asked for a butt –
'You'll be lucky' the Sergeant said, 'Fatal command structure'.
In the Cauldron the independent company fought with lonely arable courage
down to twenty and like Lilburne won't be beaten.
While over the rear Jerzy* copped it in the chest
a thousand miles from the hell of Poland to the hell of Arnhem.

February 1991

[*Polish name for John]

Disgusting Times

Across the park rule Britannia
and bare black ash buds,

Youths eaten-up with imperialism
as my jumper is by moth-worms.

Riddled with dissipation and dope
a sixteen-year-old pukes his lungs up.

Behind a patched-up terrace
bides the blue-rinse yob-widow.

St James' men take oysters with champagne,
piss-take, fart and shit.

Poets slap each other on the backs
and talk down the working-classes.

A lunatic fascist threat:
'Three fucks a day and I'll kick your head in'.

A blues singer eats her heart out,
perverted anger in my guts.

February 1991

Mike Mosley

There is a conspiracy against the social democracy of the British common people

Grey, calloused, forgotten at fifty,
he has given his all; his wiry heart,
his skilled locked fingers, his
chipped backbone, his broken welding
language, for this choking fag,
this dark blinding pint,
this scouring Irish lament.

Scorned, down for a bundle in bird,
forsaken by wives and the DHSS,
shy of nothing 'cept himself,
to this bare room, phlegm and loneliness
between stubborn slums and useless sirens.

Driven by fury to this back ward,
wasted, ulcered, unforgiving.

I start from here to make anew
the happiness of children playing
beneath heeding enduring gulls
in a wooded tempered land.

February 1991

Schizoid

Brighton and Hove without the psychology
seediness without the pip
this is a practical life
rape in heaven or tender in hell
an old woman's love
shopping on a Saturday afternoon without memory
words keen
established poets are idiots and liars,
also by definition great poets sleep in gutters
love is pure contingency
the eyes are everything

July 1991

Limehouse

Selflessness in these dirty streets
bred for and against a daring love.
Meaning is what we make of it
oppression born straight in the face.
In bleak passages and entrances
a cleaner's grit and the warmth of the wind.
A contemptuous tenderness in iron eyes.
What Pearce spoke at Rossa's grave
lives in the crevices of cold slums;
the bitter voice of liberty like the seagull
plies the crossroad as curious as starved dogs;
touches folk and they stand straight stern
as masts of ships voyaging their world.

1991

Man-Stone

Rough-hewn, treacherous to innocence,
possibilities to a rock climber's courage,
many-edged, insincere to indolence,
when he listens to the wind through the bracken
the mountain stream has worked a deep cavern
for brooding, a funnel for slow love
to the crag's top. Split-sided he works
his sex divided by earth and sky.

A sharp cerebral edge of bourgeois dissonance.
Proletarian density: rough
solidarity and lonely hubris;
below he weeps for his mate, above
scornful of language and erosion,
his bleak body mortared by prayer.

October 1991

To Bleed With Her

O anarcho Commie girl, all struggle and bleeding,
me in the asylum with my Black friend Dennis
dreaming of fags and heroin;
a little bit of freedom
in the slavery of our madness.
Her with the starlings and waning moon,
with her fierce April heart,
bleeding with the fierce womb of her lonesomeness
and the lonely wandering workman.
On windy mornings in the market street where
but to hold her hand is my life's blood.
O to share a fag on wintry evenings
in a lonely street – all iron and sleet.

February 1992

The Fisherman

Deep-tied his line to the swivel in his mind,
his eyes wracked by the ravening tide.
A strong bite on a gravelly lay, faster than
the grey of the sky; the wind trammelling
his face like the surge of Heaven.
A cold winter's day on the jetty, when
his blood meets the force of the sea and withstands
with a deep, dark hard grip in his guts.
The tog of the rod tears the lug from his heart.

June 1993

Inheritance

A song of myself
as bleak as Treblinka

A Sweetheart's kisses
with the blood of a Jewish child

A woman at dawn
caught in the blitz

A blackbird singing
and a Panzer division

The tears of my regeneration,
a murdered Polish airman

A Romany lament
for the Gulag Baptist

Hungry sex,
the Gestapo

A curious child
raped on the Russian steppe

Longing years
shot in the back

July 1993

Over the Top

You can keep Bermuda,
give me the northern hills,
a high wind
and the rain coming.

I would give up all hope
of tenderness with women
and writing a great book
to climb Liathach
in midwinter snow.

Now with that huge mystery the sea shore
with the great black-backed and the cormorant,
half-dead through schizophrenia and fags
I chance my vision from the straight and narrow
and behold a horizon of bold durable independence
with the care of women's aid and courage of Greenham
an old emphysematous Welshman walking into dusk,
a Socialism of sea-blown starward folk.

I have walked Offa's dyke with a pack
and camped on black hills to rid a royal wedding.
Now the sea is in storm and our shame cast on the beach
and we break free and grieve with the wonder of it all.

1994

Life Poem

Lovelier than Glen Torridon
than a thrush singing at dusk
than Courbet's 'Winnower'
than the solidarity of Rose and Danny
was Vivien in her youth.

April 1994

The Vixen

A vixen long through the killing night
hungers in our covert, duplicitous suburbs
for stale, dirty chips, a wounded rat.
In her earthy womb an iron litter
pulsing for moonlight across a June field.
Bitter her eyes, rusty her saliva,
she eats her menses and placenta.
Sing for her a Romany lament in an alleyway
beneath the wintry Plough's seven stars.
Oh starved outcast citizen you are alive
beyond all perception of illuded impatient people.

1999

London

City of Chaplin and MI5.
A troubled cockney girl, stranger to herself,
marrowed by a grey savage sky across the river.
Moneyed nothingness in Knightsbridge.
The walking dead, their symbols and threats,
haunt this city, driving us into underground passages
where generosity of hearts and arms are everything.
A lungful of the wind across a park
before the dawn of cockney power,
the heart of London drowned outside an 'offie'.
From a tenement a blackbird sings;
mellow the sound, sour the land.
Incendiary to the spirits
of a broken, bitter people.
Beyond our narrow classes, stilted politics,
our poverty of heart and stomach,
we are searching for sweethearts to walk on windy
October afternoons when brown golden leaves are falling.

1999

Poetry and Poverty
A Declaration

Poetry as witness.
All poetry is a poetry of hunger for the particular rather than the general.
The purpose of poetry is to create hope in desperate circumstances.
The poetry of the common people has been driven underground since 1660.
Poetry and otherness; the otherness of the common people.
When we cease to share, our language becomes a cipher,
the language of the despatch box and the popular press.
Towards a new lyricism we need to rediscover a deciduous
language, that of Gerrard Winstanley and Emily Brontë.

Cockney poetry is underground poetry expressed in Rock music;
downbeat, dissonant, demotic; e.g. The Clash, The Jam, The Free.
Celebration of the ordinary.
Nature of the city.
Metaphysics of poverty.
There can be no cockney power without cockney poetry.

1999

The Stillness

In the beginning was stillness. But for us wonder came first, for human beings. Then fear. May knew this in her blood and George dwelt on it as they sat and smoked.

Early morning was the usual time for this silence between them; a silence that lay between both and eternity.

The struggle to buy a packet of Benson's and a *Mirror* when the newsagents opened was the same struggle that May had known in bearing her children and that George had endured as a bus driver.

Their one-bedroom bungalow lay on the edge of an Oxfordshire village, down a stony lane lined with sycamore and ash trees. In front of these trees was a large meadow where children played football and cricket, and where of an evening youths wandered searching for a peace that could only be found in the stillness of their hearts.

It was with the first frost, early one November morning that George first spat blood. He was lighting a fag in the lane when he felt a sharp pain in his chest, gave a gravelly cough and spat fresh blood and phlegm into the frosty grass.

"What's wrong luv?" May asked; "I spat blood in the lane – must be the cancer"; "My ma died of TB when I was twelve", May said, rubbing his shoulders; "TB's rare in these parts nowadays", George said quietly, "and I'm of the age for cancer. Besides, I've been off my grub and they say that's a sure sign".

George bowed his head and cried briefly, then took May's outstretched hand and caressed her fingers. Lighting their fags he looked bravely at the morning light and gave a deep sigh.

1999

Life Against Death

East wind of high summer.
Old men with cider bottles,
and I suddenly an old man.

Through the slums with Jesus,
black, broken-hearted, golden Grace.

The whistling Cockney gives
his heart away at street corners
to the young 'alci': cursing, skint.

Bengali dawn
on Whitechapel waste.

The Gestapo will pass –
there shall be silence
broken by cawing crows
and the vixen's cry.

Strong as our pain is strong,
our children are.

A savage peace,
the rain over Stepney.

1999

Summer Rain

Summer rain on Stepney streets.
Dying to oneself on dirty pavements
when clouds part and sunlight floods a courtyard.
A sufi song, as ruthful as the rain.
Shit jobs for shit wages, the cockney's curse.
On their faces, a ravaged wonderful earth.

2000

Human Hope and Hackney

Roots stronger than hope in the shabby streets.
A seagull flies from mid Atlantic to the broken doors of our dreams.
Walking us to dole-poverty and aborted love.

(This November rain against dirty windows.
Suffering the morning street with the freshness of its pain.
A sweet cuppa' and a long, slow, bitter drug).

2005

Tough One

In an East End park I smoke myself to death.
Do I care or take the piss?

Fury in the heart of an old-timer;
hanging and idiocy – English fascism.

Toffs think life's a game;
the "shagging dead" I call them.

"White Power" – a cockney tragedy;
a mug of tea the colour of blood.

Freudian psychos talk about arseholes,
good folk, about saving the earth.

Will our great sea-faring nation come to this:
a Bengali lad stuck in the gut, then pissed on?

Working class internationalism as rare
and beautiful as the black redstart.

Never so happy as growing old
with a loved-one in a quiet council flat.

A low grey sky over Bethnal Green
and a cockney lass's whistled blues.

Tuesday 21 June 2005

Hillside, Llangattock

We think with our shoulders.
On the lime-quarried hillside
down a stony lane lined with ash and hazel
a poor disused chapel where
fierce hymns give men courage.
Hardship on this hillside, riven
by lime and bracken, thistle and scree.
A cold, slow rain on a cottage in the dell
mortared with the blood of quarrymen hill-farmers.
Sheep grieve above the oak wood
where a mistle-thrush storms hell.
A feral cat hunts the black redstart; so rare, so shy.
November beeches aflame, as many
fallen leaves as slain quarry men.
Resistance of pain in the chest and spat gob.
From a dry-stone wall, jenny wren's song
holier than remembrance.
Dangerous to take the sheep track at dusk.
The blessedness of February wind
through an old goat-willow.
Here men pray with their stomachs:
the gnarled upland cabbage in a broth with barley.
The language of hunger: an alcoholic's lack.
The crow and the fox pick the dead lamb clean.
Springtime in the valley and the hawthorn blooming.

August 2005

Notes on Schizophrenia

The Utopianism of the Schizophrenic

We will have our humanity by any means necessary

Is schizophrenia merely a mental illness or is it also a mystical interpretation of the universe?

Vicariousness is the emotional half of civilised life. Sometimes it seems that schizophrenia is one long inner and often inaccessible essay in vicariousness, of vicarious suffering. The selfishness of the schizophrenic is an outward reflection of the passivity of this otherness, this inaccessible suffering.

Ronald Fairbairn writes about the child taking upon her/himself the burden of badness which appears to reside in her or his objects – unconditional (libidinal) and conditional (moral) badness. As a result of this, she/he 'can have no sense of security and no hope of redemption. The only prospect is one of death and destruction'. In this analysis, Fairbairn sees only the negative side of the problem, for the sufferer seeks redemption in the spiritualising of their ego, of their inner life. Stack Sullivan quotes Ferenczi in this respect: the sufferer is seen to "permit anything to happen to his body, which has become to him as immaterial as the outer world. His whole narcissism retreats into the spiritual ego which is, so to speak, a citadel which still holds out, though outer and inner forts are lost". But there is a need to get beyond the dimensions and characterisations of post-Freudian western psychoanalysis. As Christopher Caudwell put it in his study of Freud ('Studies in a Dying Culture') – "The censor, the ego, the super-ego, the id, the Oedipus complex, and the inhibition are mind deities, like the weather deities who inhabited Greek Olympus. Freud's picture of a struggle between eternal *eros* and eternal *thanatos*, between life and death instincts, between the reality principle and the pleasure principle, is only the eternal dualism of reflective barbarians, carried over by Christianity from Zoroastrianism, and now introjected by Freud into the human mind. It represents a real struggle but in terms of a western bourgeois myth".

Schizophrenia is dissociated sexuality, the inner war between the unconscious and the conscious. Splits between hate and love, action and dreams, force and tenderness, anger and consideration, fragment the sexuality, draining the body of libidinal association and the mind of carnal coherence – whence the characteristic masturbatory fantasy life or impotence of the sufferer.

I believe this dissociation occurs because of an addiction to a memory taking place at a time of personal crisis. This causes a cybernetic short-cut. This addiction may be the result of a long period or acute episode of thalamic disintegrity and insecurity consequent on the invasion by introjection of a powerful alien will, perhaps that of a parent in an impressionable child, or that of a dead pal at war. This introjection occurs together with the values and experiences of the immediate environment; so that a post-1945 experience in a soldier's child may include the introjection of the experience of the extermination camps as well as battles and the prevalent army bullshit. At its best, the inner struggle of the schizophrenic to regain his/her individuality approaches the condition of civil war. For the alien will and the compensatory addiction have grained lives and biological forces of their own. But, using the cathexis of good inner intimate objects, the subject may make headway.

There is a vast amount I do not understand about the relationship of schizophrenia with time. However, together with the future block which Lidz writes about, there is a general speeding up of time which may be connected with the impatience of suppressed hunger.

In the future, I'd like to write about the relationship of schizophrenia with psychoanalysis, as well as more on the above sketchy hypothesis.

Finally, I'd like to expand on what I call the utopianism of the schizophrenic: his or her particular contribution to our contemporary worldview.

A schizophrenic has an existential duty towards the community in communicating by word, organisation or art his/her particular spiritual richness...

David Kessel, 1988-89

Lovelier than your modesty, this valley before me,
Deeper than mystery, holier than prayer.

"Be just and fear not"*.

David Kessel, a fragment

[Note: *this Methodist quote is outside Halifax Town Hall]

Oh dance a dance amid the field of lilies
Shrug off the aches and limits of the flesh.
Set free the searching spirit in the meadows
In the ash tree's shade we'll seek our rest.

Oh dance a dance of pain among the daffies
Clutch the blue bells strong and smelling spring.
Straddle the brook, rushing over boulders
And climb the broken gate to gain the better view.

Oh, let's walk the little bluff that tempts us yonder
Welcome the wind and soft rain on the face
The springing turf will help us on our journey
The pure hill air infuses our tired lungs.

Oh, dance a dance among the autumn bracken
With all the hues and shades the hills will glow.
And if by then mortality should beckon
I reckon it may well be time to go.

So dance a dance of life across the hilltops.
Bluebells, lambs, the daffies – all will come.
Death's but a part of life and always shall be,
And "Life's a Dream" when all is said and done.

Peggy Kessel
17 January 1985